W9-CKP-950

A QUICK GUIDE TO TELEVISION WRITING

A QUICK GUIDE TO TELEVISION WRITING

RAY MORTON

AN IMPRINT OF HAL LEONARD CORPORATION

Copyright © 2013 by Ray Morton

All rights reserved. No part of this book may be reproduced in any
form, without written permission, except by a newspaper or magazine
reviewer who wishes to quote brief passages in connection with a review.

Published in 2013 by Limelight Editions
An Imprint of Hal Leonard Corporation
7777 West Bluemound Road
Milwaukee, WI 53213

Trade Book Division Editorial Offices
33 Plymouth St., Montclair, NJ 07042

Printed in the United States of America
Book design by Mark Lerner

Library of Congress Cataloging-in-Publication Data is available upon
request.
ISBN 978-0-87910-805-2

www.limelighteditions.com

For Kate, Maddie, and Carrie Lutian

Contents

Introduction 1

Chapter 1 Dramatic Storytelling 3

Chapter 2 Dramatic Storytelling for Television 25

Chapter 3 The Teleplay Writing Process 39

Chapter 4 The Television Writing Process 47

Chapter 5 Script Format, Structure, and Length for
            Single-Camera Shows 55

Chapter 6 Script Format, Structure, and Length for
            Multi-Camera Sitcoms 71

Chapter 7 Script Format, Structure, and Length for
            Multi-Camera Shows Shot on Video 79

Chapter 8 A Few Tips 83

Chapter 9 Jobs for Television Writers 87

Chapter 10 Creating a Television Series 97

Chapter 11 Writing Other Forms of Television 103

Chapter 12 The Business of Television Writing 109

Acknowledgments 117

Introduction

Television is a medium of enormous diversity. It offers a wide array of programming, including news and commentary, talk shows, game and competition series, variety, documentaries, and reality, how-to, makeover, and clip shows.

The most popular form of television is drama (a category that includes both comedy and "serious" drama): fictional stories from a wide range of genres. This type of programming will be the main focus of this book.

All drama is scripted. The script for a television show is called a teleplay—a written blueprint that identifies all the settings and characters that will appear in the show; describes the things those characters will say and do in those settings in the precise order in which they will say and do them; and indicates the major props and effects (practical, visual, and sound) that will be required to realize these events. In aggregate, all these elements tell a dramatic story: a narrative in which a main character in pursuit of a significant goal becomes involved in a conflict that will eventually lead to a climax, a resolution, and (ultimately) a transformation. A well-written teleplay aspires to tell a tale that—after it has been interpreted, realized, and transmitted by a team of skilled artists, technicians, and craftspeople—will engage, entertain, and move an audience.

This book will teach you the basics of writing a teleplay—the essential elements, principles, and formats that, when mixed with your own imagination and creativity, will help you get started telling wonderful stories for the small screen.

CHAPTER 1

Dramatic Storytelling

All forms of dramatic writing—from stage plays to movie scripts to teleplays—are constructed from the same basic components.

THE PREMISE

The premise is the core concept of the story. It has two parts:

1. The Narrative Premise.

A basic outline of the tale to be told. The Narrative Premise incorporates the following elements:

- The Setup. The story's "hook": Two young people from feuding families fall in love; an English nobleman robs from the rich to give to the poor; a lost alien is taken in by a lonely young boy; etc.

- The Protagonist. The main character of the story (sometimes called the Hero). The Protagonist has a significant goal he or she wants or needs to achieve. That goal can be big (to save the world) or small (to save a local landmark); it can be internal (to overcome a trauma) or external (to find a buried treasure); it can be personal (to find love) or public (to stop global warming). The actions the Protagonist takes to pursue his goal drive the story forward.

At its core, drama is about transformation: In a dramatic story, the Protagonist undergoes a profound transformation as a result of his experiences in the narrative: he solves a personal problem; repairs a broken relationship; achieves fame and fortune; etc. This transformation is usually for the better, although sometimes it can be for the worse: a good cop becomes corrupt; an idealistic woman becomes cynical; a sane man descends into madness. This transformation is often called the Protagonist's "arc."

The Protagonist should always be active—he should do things rather than talk about doing things, and he should make things happen rather than simply react to events or to the actions of others.

- The Antagonist. A force that seeks to keep the Protagonist from achieving his goal. The Antagonist (sometimes called the Villain) is usually a person, but can also be a physical entity (a mountain that has to be climbed, a desert that needs to be crossed, a storm that must be survived), internal issues (phobias, a lack of confidence, an addiction), or circumstances (privation, imprisonment, oppression).

- The Central Conflict. The clash between the Protagonist, who is trying to get what he wants or needs, and the Antagonist, who is doing his or its best to prevent the Protagonist from getting what he wants or needs.
- The Dramatic Question. To create tension and suspense, every dramatic story poses a narrative question that is generated by the characters and situations and that is answered by . . .
- The Ending, which describes how the Central Conflict is ultimately resolved.

The following is the Narrative Premise of William Shakespeare's *Hamlet*: After King Hamlet of Denmark's sudden death, his son, Prince Hamlet, receives a visit from the king's ghost. The late monarch tells the prince that he was murdered by his brother, Claudius, who then took his throne and married his widow (the younger Hamlet's mother). The ghost asks the prince to avenge his murder by killing Claudius. Young Hamlet agrees, but delays action while he struggles initially to resolve his doubts about what the ghost has told him and then to find the right time to strike. The prince's hesitation gives Claudius time to plot to kill him instead. Will the son avenge his father? After Claudius's plot to poison Hamlet inadvertently kills the boy's mother instead, the prince finally takes action, slays his villainous uncle, and then succumbs himself.

The Thematic Premise.

The Thematic Premise is the point of the story—the underlying idea, "message," or "moral" the narrative is meant to convey. The Thematic Premise gives the story its purpose—it is the reason the tale is being told. Every story has a Thematic Premise—some are overt and some subtle; some are simplistic and some are complex. Some possible Thematic Premises for *Hamlet* include:

- Indecision in serious matters can have fatal consequences.
- Vengeance destroys not only the target, but also the avenger.
- Is it nobler in the mind to suffer the slings and arrows of outrageous fortune, or to take arms against a sea of troubles, and by opposing end them?

Some authors come up with the Thematic Premise for their story first and construct their Narrative Premise around it. Some come up with the Narrative Premise first and discover the Thematic Premise as they write. There is no one right way to go about it, as long as you end up with both, because without a Thematic Premise, you will have a story without a point; and without a Narrative Premise, you will have a point without a story.

THE PLOT

The plot is the structured series of events that expands the premise into a complete story. Most dramatic plots follow a very specific template—one based on the core principles of dramatic writing first set down by Aristotle in ancient Greece and refined by playwrights, screenwriters, and television writers across the ensuing millennia. This template contains all the key elements of dramatic storytelling: exposition, rising action, climax, falling action, and denouement. According to this template, a dramatic story is divided into three sections called acts, which unfold as follows:

ACT I

- The world the story takes place in is established.
- The Protagonist is introduced, and his circumstances are laid out.
- Key supporting characters, the relationships between the characters, and additional important story elements are also established.
- A crucial event sets the story in motion. This event is called the Inciting Incident.
- At the end of Act I, something happens that changes the Protagonist's situation in a very drastic way. This event is

called the Catalyst. It is also known as the First Plot Point, the First Turning Point, the First Plot Twist, the Act I Plot Twist, or the Complication.

- As a result of the Catalyst, the Protagonist develops a significant goal he becomes determined to achieve.

ACT II

- The Protagonist—usually working against some sort of tension-generating, "ticking clock" deadline—develops a plan for accomplishing his goal and then sets out to follow it.
- The Protagonist's quest to achieve his objective brings him into contact with the Antagonist, who is or becomes determined to stop the Protagonist from accomplishing his goal.
- During his quest, the Protagonist encounters a series of obstacles—primarily generated by the Antagonist—that stand between him and his objective.
- The Protagonist usually begins Act II at a disadvantage (thanks to the Catalyst), but uses his inner and outer resources—which can include special skills and abilities and help from unusual allies—to overcome these obstacles (which become bigger, more complex, and more difficult to deal with as the narrative progresses). By the midpoint of Act II, the Protagonist begins to march toward victory.

- Near the end of Act II, the Protagonist closes in on that victory. He reaches a point where it appears he is about to achieve his goal. Success seems to be within his grasp.
- At this point, something happens that once again drastically changes the Protagonist's circumstances. This event robs the Protagonist of his impending triumph and leaves him in a defeated (and often precarious) position, facing an obstacle so formidable that it appears that he will never be able to overcome it and, as result, will fail to ever accomplish his goal. This event is known as the Catastrophe. It is also known at the Second Plot Point, the Second Turning Point, the Second Plot Twist, the Act II Plot Twist, the Second Complication, and the Crash-and-Burn.

ACT III

- As Act III begins, all hope appears to be lost. The Protagonist appears to have been defeated, and it seems as though he will never be able to achieve his objective.
- At this point—when the Protagonist is at his absolute lowest—something happens that allows him or motivates him to rally.
- The Protagonist now does one of two things: he either comes up with a new plan to achieve his original objective, or else he abandons that objective and comes up with an entirely new goal (along with a plan to achieve it).

- The Protagonist sets out to put his new plan into action.
- This leads to the story's Climax—a final confrontation with the Antagonist in which the Protagonist is finally able to overcome the seemingly insurmountable obstacle— usually by defeating the Antagonist—and accomplish his goal (or fail to accomplish it, depending on the story).
- Act III concludes with the Resolution, which shows how all the story's problems are resolved and how things work out for all the characters as a result of the climax. The resolution often indicates how things are expected to go for the characters after the story ends.

The Protagonist's Arc should be incorporated into the plot as it is being constructed: The Protagonist's starting position—the place from which he will begin his transformation—should be established in Act I. This is done by dramatizing that position—usually by giving the Protagonist a problem or dilemma caused by the starting position (e.g., a workaholic's wife leaves him because he has neglected her). This problem should continue to be an obstacle for the Protagonist throughout Act II (the workaholic makes numerous attempts to win back his wife, but his devotion to his job keeps getting in the way). Eventually, events force the Protagonist to recognize he needs to change (the workaholic's wife files for divorce, causing him to finally realize he has been neglecting her). And then, at a key point in the story—sometimes at the Climax; sometimes prior to the Climax, in order to set the stage for it—the Protagonist changes (the workaholic vows to make his wife his main priority from now on). This is called the Moment of Transformation. The Protagonist's change then needs to be demonstrated (the workaholic quits his job). The impact the Protagonist's transformation will have on his life beyond the events of the story must also be demonstrated. This is usually done in the story's resolution (the workaholic and his wife reunite and live happily ever after).

Other characters in the script can also undergo transformations (e.g., a criminal Antagonist can learn the error of his ways and decide to go straight at the end of a caper movie), but their arcs should never be bigger or more significant than that of the Protagonist.

As a general guideline, Act I should run for 25 percent of the length of the overall script, Act II for 50 percent, and Act III for 25 percent. Dramatic plots can also include prologues and epilogues when necessary.

SUBPLOTS AND SCENES

Subplots

Subplots are short plotlines contained within the main story. They are constructed in the same manner as the main plot: they have three acts that include a catalyst, a catastrophe, a climax, a resolution, and an arc. Subplots are used to:

- Deliver exposition that cannot be easily introduced through the events of the main plotline
- Develop the Protagonist by showing another aspect of his character (e.g., a hard-boiled cop shows he has a soft side by helping some nuns build a new orphanage); by providing him with a reason to participate in the main story (a desperate teller decides to rob the bank that employs him to pay the enormous medical bills generated by his child's mysterious illness); or by showing the impact of the main story's events on the Protagonist's personal life (e.g., Dr. Frankenstein's obsession with reanimating the dead gets him kicked out of medical school).
- Develop a supporting character.
- Provide a counterpoint to the themes and/or action of the main story.

Scenes

To tell a dramatic story, the overall plot is broken down into individual units called scenes. A scene is a dramatization of one or more of the events that make up the story. The purpose of a scene is to advance the plot, either by adding a new link to the narrative chain or by introducing an important piece of exposition. A scene is structured like a miniature plot—it has a protagonist and an antagonist, a catalyst, central conflict, catastrophe, climax, and resolution.

ADDITIONAL STORYTELLING ELEMENTS

Action

In drama, the term *action* refers to everything the characters do. Action can be "small" (mailing a letter, talking on the phone, making a decision, etc.) or "big" (car chases, fistfights, space battles, and so on).

Dialogue

Dialogue is the words the characters say. The purpose of the dialogue is to convey information and to define character—every person in a script should speak in a unique voice, with a specific cadence, rhythm, word choice, attitude, and sense of humor that reflects his or her personality.

Images

Drama is watched by the people in the audience, so the appearance of all of the elements in a scene—the costumes, the scenery, the arrangement of props and performers—can be used to communicate information to the viewers as effectively as action and dialogue can. Devising imagery for a dramatic production is primarily the responsibility of the director and designers, but writers are certainly free to suggest images they feel will help make their points.

All dramatic stories are told using a combination of action, images, and dialogue. However, the balance between these elements changes with each medium. Because of the restricted nature of the stage itself, plays usually emphasize dialogue and "small" action, with images and "big" action taking a secondary (although still important) position. However, because the nature of cinema is much less restricted—because the camera can go practically anywhere and photograph practically anything—movies tend to emphasize images and action ("big" and "small") over dialogue.

Supporting Characters

Supporting characters are any characters who appear in the story other than the Protagonist and the Antagonist. Each supporting character must serve a specific purpose in the narrative. The most common roles that supporting characters play are:

- The Mentor. This character helps the Protagonist come into his own by introducing him to new ideas and philosophies; by teaching him new skills; by helping him develop his innate talents; by guiding him through new and unfamiliar situations; and by encouraging him to fulfill his destiny.
- The Ally. Someone who assists the Protagonist in his quest to achieve his goal. The Ally often has a special skill or talent that comes in handy during the quest.

- The Cause. A character who provides the Protagonist with a reason for pursuing his goal—a sick child who must be cured, a kidnapped love interest who needs to be rescued, a missing dog that needs to be found, etc.
- The Sounding Board. Someone—a best friend, lover, assistant, or sidekick—whom the Protagonist can talk to in order to voice his thoughts and feelings.
- The Example. Someone the Protagonist interacts with in order to show a different side of his personality—to demonstrate that the Protagonist can be warm or tough or fun or serious or resilient or so on. A love interest or a child often plays this role in a story.
- The Henchman. An assistant to the Antagonist—someone who can serve as a sounding board for the main baddie and who can do his dirty work.
- The Explainer. A resource who provides the Protagonist with information, insight, or understanding—a boss, a teacher, an expert, an advisor, a witness, or the like.
- The Supplier. A character who gives the Protagonist a special talisman, implement, or piece of equipment that will help him carry out his quest.

In addition to supporting characters, dramatic stories make use of Bit Parts—characters who have a single line or a single piece of business in a single scene.

Character Development

One of the oldest sayings in dramatic writing is that "action is character." This is true—prose can take us inside a character's mind to describe her thoughts or feelings, but drama cannot. Therefore, a character in a dramatic story is defined solely by the things he or she says and does on-stage or on-screen.

A character in a dramatic story is also defined by *how* he or she says and does things—the way in which a character behaves will tell us as much about his or her personality as the actions themselves (e.g., there is a big difference between a villain who screams a threat and a villain who delivers one without raising his voice).

Every character's personality should be unique—he or she should have specific traits, eccentricities, and attitudes that complement his or her role in the story and that make him or her as distinct from the other characters and as memorable as possible.

A character's personality should be reflected in his actions (a rough character should argue, fight, and behave recklessly; whereas a meek character should agree, compromise, and acting with care and precision).

Characters should always behave in ways that are consistent with who they are. Their personalities should not change just because it is convenient for the plot—e.g., a stupid character should not suddenly become clever just because the plot needs him to figure something out. The plot and scenes should be changed to accommodate the character, not the other way around.

All characters require strong motivation—there should be a clear and logical reason for everything a character says and does, even if it is not revealed at the time of the action.

Storytelling Devices

There are a number of different devices that dramatic writers can employ to help tell their stories:

- Suspense. This device creates tension through anticipation—by telling the audience that something significant, often something terrible or terrifying, is about to happen and then making them wait as long as possible for that thing to occur.
- Surprise. This device jolts the audience by having something unexpected happen—either out of the blue, or by first suggesting that one thing will happen, but then doing something completely different.
- Flashbacks. An expository tool in which the narrative jumps briefly back to an earlier point in the story or to a point before the story begins in order to introduce an important plot point or piece of information.
- Cutaways (a.k.a. Asides). This device serves the same purpose as a flashback, but instead of going back in time,

the story jumps briefly to another location in the world of the story.

- Nonlinear Storytelling. Presenting the events of a story in nonsequential, nonchronological order, often to create suspense or surprise.

Audiovisual forms of dramatic storytelling such as movies and television can make use of several other devices:

- Narration. A disembodied voice heard on the soundtrack that advances the story by filling in gaps in the plot, explaining the characters' motives or the meaning of a scene, and/or commenting on the action. The narrator can be a character from the story or an omniscient/omnipresent third party.
- Voice-over. The disembodied voice of a character heard on the soundtrack over the action of a scene. Voice-over is used to convey the dialogue of a character who is in a scene, but not on camera, or as a way of externalizing a character's inner thoughts.
- Montages. A series of brief events or images that are assembled into a single sequence to make a dramatic point—often to show the development of a specific skill or talent over time or to show the variety of different ways a specific story point is being implemented.

- Intercutting. A sequence that moves back and forth between two or more narrative strands or events to make a dramatic point. Often used to create suspense.
- Cards/Crawls. Two modes of printed text used to provide exposition. A card is a single block of text that appears on a blank screen or over an establishing shot. A crawl is a lengthy block of moving text that rolls up over a blank screen or an establishing shot.
- Superimposed Titles. A single line of text that appears on-screen over the action, usually to identify a date or location.

The World of the Story

Every dramatic story takes place in its own unique world. That world can be a specific time and place (prehistoric Africa, medieval France, present-day New York City); it can be a particular culture, profession, or field of endeavor (the world of Park Avenue debutantes, the world of high finance, the world of ice yachting); it can be an imaginary fantasy land (postapocalyptic New Jersey, Oz, Hell).

The story's world must be established in Act I. All relevant aspects and elements of the world—its environment, technology, manners, customs, and protocols—must be clearly explained to the audience through appropriate imagery, dramatic action, and dialogue. The more exotic and unusual the arena is, the more explanation is required. (We all know how a toaster works, but most of us probably don't understand the intricacies of high finance or experimental brain surgery.) This is especially true if the story takes place in a wholly invented fantasy world. (We're not going to know what a Fourth-Level Blondarf on the planet Lemilac is unless we are told.)

The Reality of the Story

Every dramatic story also takes place in its own unique reality (*Hamlet*, for example, takes place in a reality in which ghosts are real). That reality must be established at the very beginning—if a story takes place in a reality in which superheroes are commonplace, then we must meet a caped crusader in the opening scenes, not in the last act. Once established, a story's reality must be maintained consistently from beginning to end—if a single bullet can kill a person in Act I, then the protagonist cannot get shot twenty-seven times and live in Act III. Everything that happens in a story must be believable within its reality. Viewers will generally go along with any reality a story establishes, but if that reality is violated, they will feel cheated and will disconnect.

Exposition

Exposition is the background information—character histories; important events that occurred prior to the beginning of the plot; technical information—the audience needs to have to understand the story.

All exposition must be dramatized. Many beginning dramatic writers make the mistake of writing exposition into the text of their scripts in the same way an author would write it into a novel. For example:

JOE SMITH is standing in line at the supermarket. Joe was once a CIA agent, but he resigned after his partner and good friend Pete was killed by CYRUS, an enemy agent. Joe and Pete had captured Cyrus and were escorting him to federal prison when Cyrus killed Pete and escaped. Joe now works as an English teacher at the local high school and is engaged to Sarah, a science teacher at the same school. While waiting in line, Joe turns and sees an ELDERLY MAN join the line next to him. Although Joe can't put his finger on it, he senses something familiar about the elderly man. Suddenly, he realizes the elderly man is actually Cyrus wearing makeup that makes him look twenty years older than he really is. Joe makes the decision to capture his old nemesis.

As vital as this information is, none of it will be communicated to the people in the audience, because they can't read the script. They can only see what is happening on the stage or the screen and, in this case, all they will see is a man in line in a supermarket staring at an old guy. To communicate exposition to the audience, it must be presented in a combination of action, images, and dialogue.

The example above could be dramatized as follows:

We begin with a prologue that introduces Joe and Pete capturing Cyrus and taking him to federal prison. On the way, Cyrus kills Pete and escapes. Joe chases him, but Cyrus gets away. We can then jump forward several years and meet Joe again as he teaches his English class. After dismissal, he goes to Sarah's classroom to steal a kiss—and she asks him to go to the supermarket to pick up soda for their engagement party that night. As Joe waits in line, we can indicate that he sees some non-gray hair poking out from under the elderly man's wig, or sees a piece of the old-age makeup flake off, revealing Cyrus's unwrinkled skin beneath. Joe can then surreptitiously call his old boss, tell the boss he has found Cyrus, and announce that he is going to capture the fugitive.

All important exposition must be introduced as early in the script as possible—in Act I or at the beginning of Act II—so the audience will be able to understand and follow the narrative clearly from the get-go. Except for information that cannot be revealed until the end so as not to ruin the story (e.g., the revelation of the killer's identity and motive at the climax of a whodunit), no significant exposition should ever be introduced in Act III. By that point, a dramatic story should be racing towards its climax and taking the audience along with it. If the narrative has to suddenly stop to explain some vital point, the dramatic momentum will be lost and viewers yanked out of the tale at the very moment they should be the most engrossed in it.

Exposition should be kept to a minimum—the audience should be given only the information needed to clearly comprehend the story. Nonvital or irrelevant background should not be included in the script.

Purpose

Every element in a dramatic story must have a purpose—every character, plot point, scene, bit of exposition, and storytelling device must support the narrative, theme, or both. Any element that does not have a purpose should be removed—there should never be extraneous or irrelevant characters, story elements, or devices in a dramatic tale.

CHAPTER 2

Dramatic Storytelling for Television

TYPES OF TELEVISION DRAMA

There are three basic types of dramatic television programming:

- Series
- Miniseries
- TV Movies

In the early days of television, dramatic programs were telecast live as they were performed. Today, most dramatic programs are prerecorded (on film, on videotape, or in a digital format) and transmitted later.

SERIES

When it comes to storytelling, movies and plays are one-offs—they use a unique set of characters to tell a single, self-contained story. Some forms of television—TV movies and miniseries—are also one-offs. However, the majority of television programs are series.

A television series is a string of shows that tell numerous stories based on the same core concept, set in the same basic locations, and featuring the same set of characters. Each individual story is called an episode, and in a primetime series, a new episode usually airs once a week. The number of episodes in a series can range from as few as six to as many as twenty-four. If a program is successful, multiple series (called "seasons" in the United States) are often produced.

On American television, there are six basic types of dramatic series:

- Drama. A one-hour show, shot on sets and locations in much the same way movies are. This category encompasses multiple genres, including character-based shows, procedurals, mysteries, action, fantasy, and nighttime soap operas. Currently airing examples include: *Mad Men*, *NCIS*, *Castle*, *The Mentalist*, *Grey's Anatomy*, *Parenthood*, *Elementary*, *The Walking Dead*, *The Good Wife*, and *Game of Thrones*.

- Multi-Camera Situation Comedy. A half-hour show recorded using three or four cameras simultaneously on studio sets in front of a live audience. Currently airing examples include: *The Big Bang Theory*, *Two and a Half Men*, *Mike and Molly*, and *2 Broke Girls*.

- Single-Camera Situation Comedy. A half-hour show shot on sets and locations in much the same way movies are. Currently airing examples include: *Modern Family*, *Parks and Recreation*, and *Raising Hope*.
- Animated Situation Comedy. A half-hour show created using cel or computer-generated animation. Currently airing examples include: *The Simpsons*, *Family Guy*, and *South Park*.
- Serials (a.k.a. daytime soaps). A thirty or sixty-minute show shot on sets. Most daytime soaps play five times a week throughout the year, so many more episodes are produced for soaps than are produced for primetime series. Currently airing examples include: *General Hospital*, *Days of Our Lives*, and *The Bold and the Beautiful*.
- Sketch Shows. Thirty-, sixty-, or ninety-minute shows comprised primarily of a series of brief sketches, usually comedic, performed by a resident company of actors. Currently airing examples include: *Saturday Night Live*, *Inside Amy Schumer*, and *Key and Peele*.

STRUCTURE

All dramatic stories are structured in accordance with the classic three-act template outlined in the last chapter. However, three-act stories are not always presented in three distinct parts.

There are three-act plays in the theater, of course. There are also one-act plays, two-act plays, and sometimes even four- and five-act plays, but these designations usually have more to do with how the plays are presented than how the narratives are constructed. Plays can be long, so their performances are often broken up to give the actors a break. These breaks are called intermissions. Most plays are presented with an intermission after each act, so a one-act play has no intermission, a two-act play has one, a three-act play has two, and so on. Movies are usually shown without an intermission. (The big road show productions of the 1950s, '60s, and '70s had intermissions, but modern films do not).

Television programs that appear on pay cable channels are also presented without interruption. However, programs that appear on commercial television (broadcast and basic cable) are not. Half-hour shows on commercial television usually contain three commercial breaks; one-hour shows usually contain four or five; longer programs (TV movies and miniseries) usually average four or five breaks per hour. As a result, the scripts for commercial television programs are divided into the number of acts required to accommodate these commercial intermissions: half-hour shows have traditionally contained two acts plus a teaser (a brief prologue that comes right before or plays under the opening titles) and/or a tag (a brief epilogue that appears just before or plays under the end credits), although in recent years some half-hour shows (primarily single-camera programs) have adopted a three-act format. An hour-long show usually contains four or five acts plus a teaser and/or a tag.

No matter how many segments a dramatic story is presented in, the overall narrative is still structured according to the three-act template. A one-act play has the same narrative structure as a three-act play, but because the story itself is considerably shorter, the three parts of the narrative are presented without interruption. A two-act play also has the same narrative structure as a three-act, but the intermission is usually placed in the middle of the narrative's second act (which is a natural high point in the story—the moment when the protagonist's fortunes begin to change—and so is a good place to pause). Four- and five-act plays also tend to insert an intermission into the middle of the narrative's second act and then also attach an extended prologue and/or epilogue that are followed or preceded by additional intermissions.

In a traditional half-hour show on commercial TV, the ad breaks are usually placed between the teaser and the main narrative; in the center of the narrative's second act; and then at the end of the narrative's third act (just before the epilogue, if there is one). In a one-hour show, the breaks are usually placed between the prologue and the main narrative; at the end of the first act; in the middle of the narrative's second act; at the end of the second act; and at the end of the third act.

The challenge for television writers is to end each segment of their teleplays in a way that will compel viewers to return after the break. Options include: ending the segment with a cliffhanger (leaving the protagonist in a dangerous, potentially life-threatening situation); ending with a question ("What's behind that locked door?"); or ending on an emotional high note or low note (e.g., leaving a character feeling incredibly happy or impossibly sad).

SERIALIZED STORYTELLING

Daytime serials (a.k.a. soap operas)—daily programs featuring ongoing storylines that wind through every episode for weeks, months, and even years at a time—have been a television staple since the birth of the medium (when they were carried over from radio). However, from those early days until the end of the 1970s, the majority of primetime television series consisted of stand-alone episodes. Although the characters and basic situations were carried over from week to week, the narrative in each episode of a primetime show was usually self-contained. There were a few exceptions, of course—so-called "nighttime soaps" such as *Peyton Place* and the occasional sitcom such as *I Love Lucy* that would thread a continuing narrative (e.g., Lucy's landmark pregnancy) through an entire season—but for the most part, all the plot threads on primetime shows were wrapped up at the end of each episode, nothing was carried over, and the next week's story was entirely fresh and new.

In the early 1980s, the success of the nighttime soaps *Dallas* and *Dynasty* prompted the networks to make serials a permanent staple of their primetime lineups. During this same period, the creators of *Hill Street Blues*—a series that belonged to a genre (the cop show) that had traditionally featured stand-alone episodes—decided to tell their stories in serialized fashion. While each episode of this landmark show did contain isolated elements, the majority of every installment was devoted to servicing a collection of ongoing narratives that stretched from the beginning of the season until the end. This approach proved to be popular and caught on.

Because of these two developments, the majority of primetime shows are now serialized to some degree. Most character-driven dramas currently on the air—whether they are identified as soaps (*Revenge*) or not (*Parenthood*, *Grey's Anatomy*)—are essentially serials, with each major character given a storyline (usually called an "arc") that unfolds as the series progresses and with each episode devoted to presenting segments of those storylines. Sitcoms and one-hour genre shows such as police, medical, and legal procedurals, mysteries, action/adventures, and fantasies still feature episodes that are mostly stand-alone, but even they contain running plotlines (such as the "Will they or won't they?" romances that have become a staple of modern sitcoms).

"A" AND "B" STORIES

Episodes for primetime television series traditionally feature two plotlines in every episode:

- The "A" story is the episode's main narrative and features whichever regular character is the protagonist of that segment's primary plot, along with the other regulars, recurring characters, and guests required to support the protagonist in that storyline.
- The "B" story is a separate, minor plotline (which may or may not be connected to the "A" story) that features any regular characters who are not being used in the "A" story (all of a series' regular characters must be used in every episode, since the actors playing them are being paid for every episode). The events of the "B" story are minor compared with those in the "A" story, and the stakes are much less significant.

A good example of "A" and "B" stories occur in "The Prestidigitation Approximation," an episode of *The Big Bang Theory*. In the "A" story, Leonard's new girlfriend pressures him to break off his friendship with old girlfriend Penny, something Leonard is reluctant to do. In the "B" story,

Sheldon becomes obsessed with trying to figure out the secret behind one of Howard's card tricks.

Nighttime soaps and other heavily serialized shows have a different construction—they usually contain "A," "B," and "C" stories that are used to service their numerous ongoing narratives. In these shows, the plotlines are usually of equal importance, although one may be featured more prominently than the others in a particular episode.

CHARACTERS

One-off forms of television storytelling (TV movies, miniseries, etc.) feature the same types of characters as those in movies and plays: a protagonist, antagonist, supporting players, and bits.

Television series feature three categories of characters:

- Regulars: a group of characters who appear in every episode of the series.
- Recurring: characters who appear on a regular basis, but not in every episode.
- Guests: characters who only appear in a single episode.

When it comes to regulars, some shows feature ensemble casts in which all the characters are more or less equal and the focus of the show shifts from one member of the ensemble to another from episode to episode. Other series have a clearly defined lead character (or characters) who is (are) the focus of most of the show's episodes; the rest of the characters support the lead or leads, although every once in a while, an episode may focus on one of the supporting characters.

When it comes to show construction, the protagonist of a series changes with every episode—whichever character is the focus of a particular episode is the protagonist of that episode.

The stories told in a television series should be about the regular characters, not about guest characters—fans tune in to watch the adventures of people they know and love, not the adventures of people they've never met and will never see again (there's an old network saying: "Nobody cares about the guest star"). Guest characters can certainly be used as catalysts or foils, but they should never be used as protagonists.

CHARACTER TRANSFORMATION

As mentioned in the previous chapter, drama is about transformation—the protagonist of a dramatic story undergoes a significant change in the course of the narrative (a change brought about by the events of the narrative) and is a substantially different person at the end of the tale than he was at the beginning (e.g., Hamlet begins as an indecisive person and ends as a decisive one.)

This is true for the protagonists of movies, stage plays, and one-off television narratives. However, it has not traditionally been the case for the regular characters in a television series. With rare exception, the regulars in an ongoing show do not change who they are—at least not significantly. Regular characters in long-running series often soften or sharpen incrementally over time, but that is usually the result of a show's writers and actors choosing to emphasize or downplay a regular's existing traits to make the character play better or take advantage of the actor's unique talents, rather than the outcome of a classic dramatic transformation. In other words, while the regular's surface traits may change, his or her fundamental essence does not.

There are some very practical reasons for this. If a regular character undergoes a drastic transformation, the premise of the show may be ruined. (If Hawkeye Pierce had started obeying his superiors and following Army regulations, the core "doctors versus the brass" concept of *M*A*S*H* would have evaporated.) Also, one of the primary reasons that people become regular viewers of a television series is because they like the characters; if those characters change too drastically, the fans may lose interest and stop watching.

Still, drama requires some sort of transformation. One way for writers to satisfy this requirement is to have a regular learn some small lesson that does not fundamentally change who he or she is (e.g., *The Big Bang Theory*'s Sheldon learns to behave politely when Penny insists, even though it will never be his natural inclination to do so). Another way is have a regular undergo a transformation in circumstances rather than personality—by getting married, having a baby, landing a new job, moving into a new home, etc. A third way is to have a regular inspire a guest character to change.

ACTION, DIALOGUE, AND IMAGES

As with theatrical storytelling, the emphasis in television storytelling is primarily on dialogue and "small" action. Because TV shows are filmed with cameras in the same way movies are, imagery and "big" action are also important; but since the visual scope of television is so much more narrow than that of the cinema (due to the much smaller screen size), they are secondary.

For writers, the challenge of crafting a dialogue-driven teleplay is to use the dialogue to propel the story without allowing it to become overly expository or pedantic.

In serialized shows, dialogue is often used to recap important events that have happened in previous episodes ("Remember when you collapsed during the cotillion and had to have emergency brain surgery?"). The challenge here is to pen dialogue that gets this information across without sounding as stiff and awkward as my example.

PRACTICALITY

Practicality is a very important aspect of writing for television. Compared with movies, TV programs have limited budgets and must be shot on tight and relatively inflexible schedules. Therefore, television shows can not have as many scenes, sets, locations, and effects as movies do. Writers need to keep this in mind as they craft their stories and teleplays.

When writing for a television series, writers should use the show's regular sets as much as possible, since they are already standing and paid for. Likewise, they should use the series' regular characters as much as possible, since guest characters require guest actors, who add to the budget. Most shows only budget for one or two extra sets and one or two guest stars per episode, so keep this in mind when developing your stories.

Time is also an issue. Sans commercials, a thirty-minute show runs about twenty minutes, and a sixty-minute show runs about forty-five minutes. This is another reason to limit the number of scenes and characters in a teleplay, because trying to cram too many elements into such a brief amount of time can result in a mishmash.

CHAPTER 3

The Teleplay Writing Process

There are nine basic steps to writing a teleplay:

1. Come Up with a Good Idea

A good idea for a teleplay is one with a compelling hook—a core concept that will grab an audience, pull them into the story, and keep them engaged for the running time of the piece. A good hook is clever, interesting, reasonably original, and entertaining (meaning it is funny, dramatic, thrilling, informative, thought-provoking, or inspiring, depending on the kind of story you want to tell).

A good idea for a teleplay is one that can be dramatized effectively—meaning it can be told through a combination of action, images, and dialogue (concepts for narratives driven primarily by a character's inner thoughts and feelings are not good candidates for dramatization)—and takes into consideration the constraints of the medium (i.e., it focuses on characters and dialogue, rather than on big action and visual spectacle).

If you are writing a teleplay for a series, then a good idea is one that fits the concept, format, and style of the show and that makes effective use of its existing characters and sets.

2. Assemble Your Tools

Most scriptwriters today work on a computer (often employing specialized software such as Final Draft, which provides templates for all forms of dramatic writing, including a wide variety of teleplays). But a good number still prefer to use a pen and paper, and a few even continue to use typewriters.

3. Write an Outline

The outline is the written skeleton of your story—the document in which you lay out the plot and develop your narrative.

Some scriptwriters create very simple outlines—they make a list of the basic story points (a.k.a. "beats") called a step sheet or a beat sheet, or they jot down each story point on an individual index card and then shuffle the cards around until they find a satisfactory shape for their tale. Others craft very thorough outlines, with each scene in the narrative fleshed out in detailed prose, often incorporating key snippets of dialogue. Most professional television writing assignments require writers to create and submit the latter type of outline.

As you write the outline, you should develop your story in accordance with the principles of dramatic and television storytelling outlined in Chapters 2 and 3—creating a three-act tale (even if you're telling it in two or four or five acts) featuring an active protagonist (who, if you're writing a teleplay for an existing series, must be one of the regulars) pursuing a strong, clear goal whose actions continually drive a plot filled with suspense, surprise, and solid supporting characters ever forward toward an exciting climax and satisfying resolution. Your tale should adhere to the parameters of the type of television program you are writing, and to the specific format and episode structure of the particular program your script is meant for. If you are creating a teleplay for commercial TV, it should incorporate the appropriate ad breaks.

4. Write a Rough Draft

The rough draft is the first full iteration of your story in script form. No matter how finely honed your outline and treatment are, the rough draft is usually a messy document—the narrative and storytelling are often a bit awkward; key components can be underdeveloped, illogical, or unclear; and there are frequently too many ideas, too many characters, and too much plot. That's OK—the purpose of writing the rough draft is not to produce a finished piece of work. It is simply to get your ideas down on paper—to generate the raw material from which the final script will be created.

5. Do Your First Rewrite

"Writing is rewriting," the saying goes, and it's true—rewriting is how you transform the raw material of the rough draft into a viable teleplay. It is the process by which the story and theme are focused, rudimentary characters and dialogue are transformed into flesh-and-blood people, and speech and extraneous elements are pared away. Some writers do a single extensive revision to their initial draft; others do numerous passes. There's no right way, other than to do whatever you have to do to make your script as good as it can be.

6. Get Feedback

Once you have produced a solid rewrite of your teleplay, it is a good idea to get some feedback on your work.

Obtaining good feedback is a key part of the writing process. Your script's primary task is to communicate your creative concepts and ideas to others—first to the brass (the producers, studio, and network); then to the creative team (the actors, directors, technicians, and craftspeople) tasked with bringing the piece to the screen; and finally to an audience—so it is vital to assess how good a job your teleplay is doing in getting your points across.

The most direct way to get feedback is to give your script to a few fellow writers or others whose taste and judgment you respect and whom you can trust to give you an honest opinion. (Giving it to multiple readers is crucial, because one person's opinion is just that, but if several people have the same reaction—good or bad—to the same points, then you have a much better idea of where you stand.) Once your readers have completed their task, ask them questions: What parts of the teleplay did they like? What parts did they have problems with? Why didn't those parts work for them? Was anything in the piece confusing or unclear? Did they care about the characters? Was there any element they wanted more of? Less of? Was the ending satisfying? When analyzing the responses, look for points of consensus—if most of your readers agree that a specific part of the teleplay works well, then you're probably in good shape. If most have a problem with a specific part, then you've probably got more work to do.

The most important thing to do when you receive feedback is to listen to it, especially if it is negative. While it is certainly difficult to hear that something you've worked so hard on is not 100 percent perfect, it's imperative that you not become defensive or resistant, because such attitudes will get in the way of the ultimate goal: to produce the best teleplay possible.

7. Do a Second Rewrite

Use the feedback you've received as a guide to help you revise your material—to enhance what works and to fix any problems. As you rewrite, be ruthless—don't just tweak the script here and there, but be brave enough to tear it apart: revising where necessary, rethinking where necessary, and cutting where necessary, even if it means eliminating bits you really love. (In such instances, it's best to remember the old writing adage: "In order to succeed, you must first kill all your darlings.")

8. Do It All Again

Repeat Steps 5 and 6 as many times as necessary until the script is as good as it can be.

9. Prepare a Presentation Draft

This is the first draft you will show to the professional world—the version you will deliver to agents, producers, studios, and networks. When working on a contracted scriptwriting assignment, the presentation draft is your official "first" draft—the one you turn in to the people who hired you. (Most contracted assignments for movies and television require the writer to produce an outline or treatment, followed by a first draft, and then—after receiving notes from the producers, studio, and network—a revised second draft. Any work beyond that second draft usually requires a new contract and additional payment.)

When preparing your presentation draft, proofread the piece carefully—double-and triple-checking the spelling, grammar, and formatting—from page one to page last. It is important to do this so that the teleplay looks professional and so there will be nothing in the piece to distract readers or prevent them from focusing on the content. If you're not confident of your skills in this area, consider using a professional proofreader because, as the saying goes, "You never get a second chance to make a first impression."

CHAPTER 4

The Television Writing Process

LONGFORM

The scripts for TV movies are usually written in the same fashion as those for movies: a writer is commissioned (by a producer, studio, or network) to write a teleplay based on a specific subject. The writer prepares an outline or treatment and then writes a first draft and a revision. If more work is required, the writer may be contracted to do additional drafts or an entirely new writer might be hired. After sufficient revisions have been made, the script is put into production.

Miniseries can be written in the same fashion, with one writer crafting the teleplay for all the episodes in the piece. For some miniseries, though, a different writer is hired to write each individual episode—*QB VII* (1974), the first miniseries on U.S. television, was written by a single screenwriter (Edward Anhalt), as were 1976's *Rich Man, Poor Man* (Dean Riesner) and 2008's *John Adams* (Kirk Ellis). However, 1998's

From the Earth to the Moon and 2001's *Band of Brothers* were penned by multiple scribes.

SERIES

The scripts for an ongoing television series are generated primarily by the show's writing staff.

In the early days of TV, most shows did not have a large number of writers on staff—the majority had a head writer (sometimes called the writing producer and today called the showrunner) and perhaps a story editor, both of whom might write a few episodes. However, most segments were generated by freelance writers (from original ideas of their own or from ideas assigned to them by the head writer). Today, though, most series maintain a sizable writing staff.

Led by the showrunner, the members of the staff usually work together to develop the various narrative arcs that will thread through the series in a season and then break those arcs down into however many segments will be needed for the number of episodes that will be produced that year. The staff then generates story ideas and frequently even entire outlines for individual episodes.

On some shows, these concepts are then divvied up among the individual staff members, who go off and—under the supervision of the showrunner—transform them into detailed outlines (if the staff has not already done so), first drafts, and revisions. Other shows—primarily sitcoms—are "room written": all the staff members gather in a single room and write each episode together line by line.

(Note: Although staffers do write the majority of a series' episodes, the Writers Guild of America requires all shows produced by signatories to its Minimum Basic Agreement—which include any show produced by all the major U.S. studios, networks, and television production companies—to give a certain number of assignments to freelance writers each season. See Chapter 5 for further details.)

If the showrunner—the person responsible for the creative direction of the show—is unhappy with a writer's final draft, he or she has the option to give it to another staffer to revise. Most freelance scripts are rewritten by a staff member, since the staffers obviously have a better understanding of the show's nuances than an outside writer does.

Once the writers have completed their final drafts, all the scripts are then usually rewritten (sometimes lightly, sometimes heavily) by the showrunner so he or she can fix any remaining problems and give all the episodes in the series a consistent tone and voice.

The writer who pens the original story outline and initial drafts of the script for a particular episode usually receives the "Written By" credit for that episode. If the outline is written by one scribe and the teleplay by another, then the writer of the outline receives a "Story By" credit and the author of the script receives a "Teleplay By" credit. If any subsequent writer makes a significant contribution to the teleplay writer's script—if the new writer drastically changes the story and/or the characters in some substantial way—then she or he will usually split the "Teleplay By" credit with the original writer, who will then be given a "Story By" credit to signify that he or she was the originator of the piece. If the final draft of the script is primarily the work of the subsequent writer, then the original scribe may only receive a "Story By" credit, and the "Teleplay By" credit will go to the subsequent writer. Since the Writers Guild of America will only allow a maximum of three writers (or writing teams) to receive a "Teleplay By" credit, for room-written shows, half the staff will frequently take a "Story By" credit and the other half a "Teleplay By" credit.

(Another note: The final credits on any teleplay created under the jurisdiction of the Writers Guild of America are officially determined by the guild. When an episode is finished, the production company notifies the WGA and all participating writers of the credit it plans to put on the episode. If the writers all agree with the credit, then it is accepted by the guild and placed on the program. If any of the writers object, the matter is sent to arbitration, where a team of select WGA members with no connections to the project reviews all drafts of the story outline and teleplay and determines the final credit based primarily on the percentage of material each writer is determined to have contributed to the final script. This is a crucial process not just for vanity reasons, but also because lucrative residual payments are tied to receiving an on-screen credit.)

On single-camera shows, the showrunner's draft is usually the one that is shot. On a multi-camera sitcom, the showrunner's draft is just the halfway point on the road to a final script.

Single-camera television shows are shot scene by scene over an approximately one-week production schedule. In contrast, multi-camera shows are recorded all at once in front of a live studio audience on the final day of a five-day production schedule.

- On the first day of the production schedule, the cast, director, and writing staff gather for what is called the "table read": the team sits around a large table, and the actors read the script aloud from beginning to end, as the writers note which lines and scenes are working and which are not. Following the table read, the actors go to the set and begin rehearsing while the writers fix the identified problems. The revised script pages are distributed to the director and cast, and the next day, rehearsal continues.

- At the end of the second day, a run-through is held on set—the actors perform the show from beginning to end so that the writers can see what the piece looks like "on its feet." After the run-through, the writers revise the script again to fix anything that still isn't working. (If the problems are major, it is not uncommon for scenes and sometimes even entire acts to be rewritten from scratch or thrown out entirely and replaced with something entirely new.) The revisions are distributed, and the next day, rehearsal continues.

- At the end of the third day, the process is repeated—there's another run-through and additional rewriting.

- On the fourth day, the cameras are brought onto the set, and the various shots and camera moves are worked out. By now, the script is (hopefully) close to final, but following a dress and camera rehearsal (with the actors in full costume and the camera operators practicing their moves), more rewriting is done if it is deemed necessary.

- On the fifth day, the show is performed and recorded in front of an audience. Shows shot on film are usually recorded once, following a final dress and camera rehearsal. Shows shot on videotape or digitally are usually recorded twice—the final rehearsal is recorded (in front of one audience) in the late afternoon, and the show itself is shot that evening (in front of a second audience). Any last-minute line adjustments are made between the final rehearsal and the evening performance.

SKETCH SHOWS

The individual bits on a sketch show are usually dreamed up and written by the staffers and then pitched to the showrunner, who selects the pieces that will appear in a given episode. The scripts for sketches on single-camera shows (such as *Key and Peele*) are polished ahead of shooting, while the scripts for sketch shows that are recorded (or broadcast live) in front of a studio audience (such as *Saturday Night Live*) are usually refined throughout a rehearsal period in the same fashion as scripts for multi-cam shows.

The writing staff of a sketch show is also responsible for creating the program's connective material: host introductions and monologues, interstitial pieces, and so on.

SERIALS

On a daytime soap opera, the head writer (or co-head writers—many shows have more than one) devises the overall storylines for a specific period of time (three months or six months or longer) and then writes them up in a summary called a *long-term story document*.

This document is given to outline writers (a.k.a. breakdown writers), who break the overall storylines down into individual episodes and then prepare detailed, scene-by-scene outlines for these episodes. The outlines are then handed off to the show's script writers, who pen the dialogue for each segment. Each outline writer and each script writer works on a single episode at a time.

The completed teleplays are given to the show's script editor, who polishes them to ensure that all of the episodes have a consistent tone and voice.

CHAPTER 5

Script Format, Structure, and Length for Single-Camera Shows

One-hour dramas, half-hour single-camera situation comedies, half-hour animated situation comedies, single-camera sketch shows, TV movies, and miniseries all use the same basic script format (which is essentially the same one used for feature film screenplays). Each series has its own unique formatting quirks (and if you are writing for an existing show, you should obtain copies of scripts from that program and study them, so you can conform your work to the show's specific approach), but in general:

Teleplays are written in 12-point Courier font with a 1.5-inch margin on the left and a 1-inch margin on the right.

All teleplays for single-camera shows begin with:

FADE IN:

This is followed by the first Scene Heading, a.k.a. Scene Slug. The heading tells us if the scene takes place inside—INT. (for "interior")—or outside—EXT. (for "exterior"); the name of the location; and whether the scene occurs during the day or at night. The heading is always written in all caps:

INT. UNION STATION - NIGHT

   or

EXT. THE WHITE HOUSE - DAY

   A new slug is used every time there is a change in location (even if it is only from one room in a building to another room in the same building) or time.

   When characters move from one location to an adjoining location in real time, the DAY/NIGHT segment of the second heading is replaced by the term CONTINUOUS:

INT. BEDROOM -- NIGHT

Mary is asleep in bed. Suddenly, she hears glass breaking (O.S.) coming from the living room. Concerned, Mary gets out of bed and tiptoes carefully into the

```
INT. LIVING ROOM -- CONTINUOUS
```

```
where she sees a MASKED FIGURE standing in
front of the broken bay window, holding a
machete.
```

The heading is followed by the *action line* (a.k.a. stage directions). This is the text of the scene—a written description of the dramatic action that occurs in the specified location. The action line indicates which characters are present when the scene begins, which ones enter, and which ones exit. It details what the characters do in the scene, the props that they do it with, and any other relevant action or effects. The first time a character appears in a script, his or her name is written in all caps. Important props, significant sound and visual effects, and important bits of action are also written in caps.

```
FONZIE enters the garage. He crosses to his
MOTORCYCLE, which is covered with a TARP.
Fonzie whips off the tarp, jumps on the mo-
torcycle, and kick-starts the engine. Pop-
ping a wheelie, he zooms out of the garage.
```

When a character speaks, his or her name is written in caps and placed at the 3.5-inch mark. Parentheticals—directions indicating how the speech is to be performed—are placed on the following line at the 3-inch mark. The dialogue itself is written below in a 3-inch wide, single-spaced column starting at the 2.5-inch mark.

                        HAMLET
                      (pensive)
               To be, or not to be: that is the
               question. Whether 'tis nobler in
               the mind to suffer the slings and
               arrows of outrageous fortune. Or,
               to take arms against a sea of
               troubles, and by opposing end them.

If the dialogue is narration or a voice-over, place a (V.O.) next to the character's name:

                    SYDNEY (V.O.)
               It was the best of times, it was
               the worst of times.

If the character who speaks is part of the scene, but does not appear on camera (e.g., if he or she is in another room), place an (O.S.) —for "off-screen"—next to the character's name.

```
                    GRANDMA (O.S.)
        Tommy? Is that you?
```

If you want to superimpose a title on the scene, use a partial slug as follows:

```
SUPER TITLE: New York City, 1933
```

Cards are written in similar fashion:

```
CARD: Once upon a time, a young princess was
born to the royal family of Spontania. When
the princess was sixteen, her mother died and
her father remarried. The new queen was jeal-
ous of her stepdaughter's beauty and hired an
evil huntsman to kidnap the young girl and
lock her away in a remote tower. The princess
remained a prisoner for many years, until one
day a young prince happened by.
```

Crawls are formatted in the same style as dialogue:

```
                    CRAWL
        In the last days of the World
        War II, the OSS smuggled a group
        of rocket scientists out of Nazi
```

```
         Germany and brought them to New
         York, where they were put to work
         on the most powerful weapon ever
         conceived.
```

On occasion, a close-up of a specific prop or action is required to make a story point. This is called an "insert" and is scripted as follows:

```
INT. BANK VAULT - DAY

The teller leads Mrs. Smith into the vault
and over to a bank of safe-deposit boxes. The
teller unlocks one, slides it out, and opens
it. Mrs. Smith looks inside.

INSERT - SAFE-DEPOSIT BOX

An enormous diamond rests on a bed of cash.

BACK TO SCENE

Mrs. Smith reaches into the box, pulls out
the diamond, and holds it to the light. It
sparkles.
```

When a scene is finished, we transition to the next scene. In years past, the transition

```
                                        CUT TO:
```

was used after every scene to indicate an immediate chronological move from one scene to another. However, it is no longer used because the transition is assumed (a story will cut from one scene to the next whether the script tells it to or not) and eliminating it saves valuable page space.

To indicate that time has gone by between the end of the first scene and the beginning of the second, the transition

```
                                    DISSOLVE TO:
```

is used. To indicate that a considerable period of time has elapsed between Scene 1 and Scene 2, use

```
                                        FADE OUT:
FADE IN:
```

Montage sequences are initiated with a partial heading, followed by the component scenes:

MONTAGE:

EXT. FOREST -- DAY

NOAH pours some seed into the bottom of a
crude wooden birdcage. TWO BIRDS fly into the
cage. Noah closes the cage's gate, capturing them.

EXT. SAVANNAH -- DAY

Standing on a ladder, Noah ties a rope around
the neck of a GIRAFFE. Using the rope as a
leash, Noah leads the giraffe over to a tree
where a SECOND LEASHED GIRAFFE is tethered.
Untying the tethered giraffe, Noah then leads
both animals off into the distance.

EXT. DRY DOCK -- DAY

Using a peeled banana as bait, Noah entic-
es TWO CHIMPANZEES toward a massive ARK. We
can see the previously gathered giraffes and
birds on the deck of the ship, alongside DOZ-
ENS OF PAIRS OF OTHER ANIMALS. Rain clouds
gather in the distance.

END MONTAGE

Intercut sequences are laid out in similar fashion:

INTERCUT:

EXT. APARTMENT BUILDING -- NIGHT

Doug leaves his building and walks to the corner.

EXT. BRIDAL SHOP -- NIGHT

Katya exits the store, locks the door behind
her, and walks to the corner.

EXT. CORNER OF FIFTH AVENUE AND 32ND STREET
-- NIGHT

Doug turns onto Fifth Avenue walking north.
He is looking down at his phone.

EXT. CORNER OF FIFTH AVENUE AND 33RD STREET
-- NIGHT

Katya turns onto Fifth Avenue walking south.
She is looking down at her phone.

```
EXT. FIFTH AVENUE -- NIGHT

Both focusing on their phones and not looking
where they are going, Doug and Katya collide
in the center of the block

END INTERCUT
```

After the final scene of the story is concluded, the script
ends with one last

```
                                        FADE OUT:
```

If the teleplay is divided into acts, then each act should
begin with a centered indicative heading at the start of each
act prior to the initial FADE IN:

```
                      ACT ONE
```

```
FADE IN:
```

Teasers and tags should be similarly identified:

```
                      TEASER
```

```
                       TAG
```

At the end of each act, the FADE OUT is followed by another centered indicative heading:

FADE OUT:

END OF ACT ONE

The next act begins at the top of the next page.

The end of the show should be indicated with a final heading following the end of the last act.

END OF ACT FOUR

END OF SHOW

To see how it all lays out, here is a brief sample of a properly formatted single-camera teleplay:

ACT ONE

FADE IN:

EXT. MANHATTAN GENERAL HOSPITAL - DAY

An establishing shot of the hospital.

                    DR. TENNANT (V.O.)
          Tuesday is my favorite day of the
          week. It's always so quiet and
          dull. Nothing exciting ever happens
          on a Tuesday.

SUPER TITLE: Tuesday, June 24

INT. MANHATTAN GENERAL - EMERGENCY ROOM - DAY

The waiting room is packed with sick and in-
jured PEOPLE. We see damage everywhere—broken
legs, shot arms, stabbed stomachs. There's
a lot of screaming and a lot of blood. The
E.R. PERSONNEL do their best to attend to the
overwhelming horde as ANGRY PATIENTS demand
assistance.

DR. CHRIS TENNANT, dressed in his street
clothes and nursing a cup of wake-up coffee,
enters from the street. Still half-asleep, he
is shocked to see all of this chaos.

NURSE MCCOY runs past. Tennant stops her.

                          DR. TENNANT
          What's going on, McCoy?

                          NURSE MCCOY
          Oh, Doctor, I'm so glad you're
          here. There were two gang fights
          and a bus accident, a construction
          crane collapsed on 54th Street,
          and Dr. Baker just called in sick.
          We're overwhelmed.

                          DR. TENNANT
          I'll be in six.

Dropping his coffee in a nearby trash can,
Tennant runs down the hallway and turns into

INT. EXAM ROOM 6 - CONTINUOUS

He grabs a white doctor's smock off a hook on
the wall, dons it, and turns toward a patient
sitting on the exam table: a YOUNG TOUGH with
a knife sticking out of his shoulder.

MONTAGE:

INT. EXAM ROOM 6 - DAY

Tennant treats a GANGBANGER with a gunshot wound.

INT. EXAM ROOM 6 - DAY

Tennant puts a YOUNG WOMAN's leg into a cast.

INT. EXAM ROOM 6 - DAY

Tennant stitches up a gash on the forehead of a DAZED MAN holding a hardhat.

END MONTAGE

INT. EXAM ROOM 6 - NIGHT

An exhausted Tennant lies on the exam room table. Nurse McCoy enters, carrying a cup of coffee. She hands it to him. He sits up and begins to sip it.

```
                        DR. TENNANT
              (weary)
        Well, so much for quiet and dull.


                                    FADE OUT:


              END OF ACT ONE
```

STRUCTURE AND LENGTH

A one-hour drama on commercial television usually has four, five, or six acts along with a teaser and/or a tag (once again, study the show you are writing for to determine its specific construction). One-hour dramas on pay television generally do not have act breaks. One-hour teleplays should be approximately 60 pages long. (Dialogue-heavy scripts can run a little longer; action-heavy scripts should run a little shorter.)

Thirty-minute single-camera and animation situation comedies on commercial television usually have two or three acts plus a teaser and/or a tag. Thirty-minute shows on pay TV generally do not have act breaks. Teleplays for these shows should be approximately 30 pages long. (Once again, dialogue-heavy scripts can run a little longer; action-oriented pieces should run a little shorter.)

A two-hour TV movie on commercial television usually has between eight and twelve acts, depending on the network. TV movies on pay cable do not have act breaks. A script for a two-hour TV movie on commercial television should be approximately 90 pages long. A script for a two-hour TV movie on pay cable should be 90–110 pages long.

A miniseries on commercial television usually has four, five, or six acts per hour, depending on the network. Miniseries on pay television generally do not have act breaks. The teleplay for a miniseries should be approximately 60 pages long per hour.

CHAPTER 6

Script Format, Structure, and Length for Multi-Camera Sitcoms

Thirty-minute multi-cam situation comedies on commercial television usually have two or three acts plus a teaser and/or a tag. Multi-cam sitcoms do not usually run on pay cable, but if they do, they do not have act breaks. Teleplays for these shows should be approximately 35–40 pages long.

As with single-camera scripts, multi-cam teleplays are written in 12-point Courier font with a 1.5-inch margin on the left and 1-inch margin on the right. Dialogue margins are also the same.

Each act in a multi-cam teleplay begins with a centered indicative heading:

ACT ONE

Each scene also begins with a centered indicative heading. Multi-cam sitcoms usually have three or four scenes per act, and each scene is lettered rather than numbered:

SCENE A

or just

A

Followed by an underlined:

FADE IN:

Scene headings are underlined, and the names of all the characters who appear in the scene are indicated underneath, in caps and parentheses:

INT. BILL'S APARTMENT -- DAY
(BILL, ANDREW, TOM)

The action lines/stage directions are written in caps. The first time a character or an important prop are introduced in the script, they are underlined. Character entrances and exits are also underlined:

ANDREW AND TOM ARE SITTING ON THE COUCH WATCH-
ING TELEVISION. BILL ENTERS FROM THE KITCHEN
CARRYING A BOWL OF POTATO CHIPS AND CROSSES
TO THE COUCH.

Dialogue is double-spaced:

                        BILL
        Does anyone want any—

                        ANDREW
                (cuts him off)
        Shhh! This is the best part of the
        movie. This is the scene where
        Darth Vader reveals that he's Han
        Solo's uncle.

If the action of a scene moves from one set to another without stopping, the move from one set to another is indicated with the following:

RESET TO:

At the end of a scene, transition to the next scene with an underlined

                                        CUT TO:

        or

                                    DISSOLVE TO:

At the end of each act, there is a:

<u>FADE OUT:</u>

And an:

<u>END OF ACT ONE</u>

And at the end of the show, there's an:

<u>END OF SHOW</u>

Voice-overs (V.O.), off-screen dialogue (O.S.), and montage sequences are formatted in the same fashion as they are in single-camera scripts.

Multi-camera shows do not usually use supered titles, cards, crawls, or inserts.

To see how it all lays out, here is a brief sample of a properly formatted multi-camera teleplay:

<u>ACT ONE</u>

<u>SCENE A</u>

<u>FADE IN:</u>

INT. MAIN OFFICE — DAY
(KATHY, NANCY, RICH, KEN, CLAIRE (O.S.))

KATHY IS WORKING AT HER DESK. RICH IS DELIV-
ERING THE MAIL, AND KEN IS IN THE KITCHEN
AREA MAKING COFFEE. THE ELEVATOR DOOR OPENS
AND NANCY ENTERS, SOAKING WET.

                    KATHY
          What happened to you?

                    NANCY
          What happened to me is that I
          listened to that stupid weatherman
          on WWXR this morning who said it
          was going to be sunny and bright
          this morning, so I didn't bother to
          bring my umbrella.

                    KATHY
          I never listen to that guy. He's
          all wet.

> NANCY

And now, unfortunately, so am I.

SHE CROSSES TO HER OFFICE AND <u>EXITS TO</u>

> <u>RESET TO:</u>

<u>INT. NANCY'S OFFICE - CONTINUOUS</u>

<u>NANCY ENTERS</u> AND CROSSES TO THE DESK. LOOK-
ING FOR SOMETHING TO DRY HERSELF WITH, SHE
GRABS SOME PAPERS AND BEGINS BLOTTING HER
HAIR. KATHY ENTERS.

> KATHY

Well, I'm glad you made it.
Claire's been looking for you all
morning.

> NANCY

Oh god. Whatever you do, don't tell
her I'm here.

                         CLAIRE (O.S.)
        Nancy? Are you in there?

HEARING HER VOICE, NANCY AND KATHY BOTH
FREEZE. AS THEY EXCHANGE LOOKS, WE:

                                    FADE OUT:

                    END OF ACT ONE

CHAPTER 7

Script Format, Structure, and Length for Multi-Camera Shows Shot on Video

In the pre-digital era, soap operas and many sitcoms and sketch shows were shot using multiple cameras and recorded on videotape. These programs used a different script format from that used by multi-cam series shot on film. Although videotape itself is largely a thing of the past—most programs once recorded on tape are now shot on high-definition video—soaps, some sketch shows, and the (very) rare sitcom still employ the video script format.

The video script format has some similarities to that used for filmed multi-cam shows: teleplays are written in 12-point Courier font, most elements are underlined, the action lines/ stage directions are written in caps, and the dialogue is double-spaced. However, there are some significant differences as well: all the elements are aligned with the left margin, the action lines are in parentheses and are usually double-spaced, and the text only occupies the left half of the page.

Here is a sample page to show what this format looks like:

ACT ONE

SCENE ONE

FADE IN:

INT. THE OVAL OFFICE - DAY

(THE PRESIDENT ENTERS AND LOOKS AROUND.)

                    PRESIDENT
          Hello? Is anybody in here?

(THE PRESIDENT HEARS A GIGGLE. HE MOVES AROUND
THE ROOM, LOOKING FOR WHOEVER ISSUED IT. HE
LOOKS BEHIND THE COUCH.)

                    PRESIDENT
          Hello?

(THERE'S NO ONE THERE. HE LOOKS BEHIND A
CHAIR.)

                    PRESIDENT
          Gotcha!

(THERE'S NO ONE THERE, EITHER. HEARING ANOTH-
ER GIGGLE, HE CROSSES TO THE RESOLUTE DESK.
LOOKING UNDERNEATH, HE FINDS HIS SIX-YEAR-OLD
GRANDDAUGHTER ARIEL HIDING IN THE FOOTWELL.)

                    ARIEL
               (giggling)
          Surprise!

                    PRESIDENT
               (feigns surprise)
          Oh my!

                    ARIEL
          Hi Grandpa!

                    PRESIDENT
          How did YOU get past the Secret
          Service?

(HE PICKS HER UP AND TICKLES HER.)

FADE OUT

END OF ACT ONE

Half-hour soap operas on commercial television usually have a teaser and two or three acts. Teleplays should be approximately 40 pages long.

One-hour soap operas on commercial television usually have a teaser and four, five, or six acts. Teleplays should be approximately 55 pages long.

Half-hour sitcoms on commercial television usually have two or three acts plus a teaser and/or a tag. Teleplays should be approximately 45 pages long.

CHAPTER 8

A Few Tips

Teleplays should include a list of the characters who appear in the story (if the teleplay is for an episode of a series, it should list both regular and guest characters) and a list of the sets and locations. Both of these lists should be placed in the beginning of the script.

The action lines/stage directions in a teleplay should be written in a clean and simple style—avoid fancy, flowery wording. A teleplay is not literature; it does not derive its effectiveness from the way the author uses language. It is a descriptive document, and so its words should be used to provide as clear and direct a presentation of the action as possible. Therefore:

```
It is a bright, sunny day.
```

is preferable to

```
The scene is illuminated by a thousand rays
of yellow brilliance that are raining down
```

```
from the flaming orb burning fiercely in the
endless field of azure that spreads out in all
directions high above the field.
```

Do not attempt to direct the show on paper. It is your job to tell the story. It is the job of the director (in collaboration with his or her creative team) to interpret it. Therefore:

- Except for establishing shots (which are a storytelling tool rather than a directorial one) do not write specific shots (close-ups, long shots, etc.), camera angles, or camera moves into the script—the director will determine these things in conjunction with the cinematographer.
- Avoid excessive use of inserts.
- Do not describe your characters in elaborate detail ("Lance is five feet, three inches tall, with red hair, green eyes, freckles, and a mole on his left cheek"). The director will cast the actor he or she feels is most suitable for the role, whether that actor matches your physical description or not. It is better just to provide a general but evocative impression of a character ("Dr. House is brilliant but cantankerous"; "Lady Mary is a beautiful but icy aristocrat") and leave it at that.
- Likewise, do not describe sets in intricate detail—you do not need to indicate the colors of the rugs and the patterns on the wallpaper and the precise number of chairs and tables

and curtains and wineglasses. Give a general impression of
the place ("a run-down waterfront bar") and let the production designer take it from there. Standing series sets do not
need to be described because they will always be the same.

- Avoid excessive use of parentheticals—actors don't like
  to be told how to say their lines, and directors will ignore
  them.

- Do not call for ad-libbing—that's for the director to do
  if he or she wants to.

Write the script in "master scene" format: a heading followed by a simple description of the action and the dialogue.

While is wise to avoid flowery language in the action
lines/stage directions, it is important to detail every physical action a character in the script performs. Many novice
scriptwriters tend to summarize the action: "Pete fixes the
car." These summaries are too general—they can't be acted
or photographed. Instead, make the action as specific as
possible: "Pete opens the hood and examines the engine.
Picking up a screwdriver, he reaches in and tightens a screw
on the engine block," and so on.

When writing dialogue:

- Don't summarize conversations—e.g., "They discuss the
  history of Western Europe." Instead, write out every
  word you want the characters to say.

- Don't spell accented dialogue or dialogue spoken in dialect phonetically. No matter how well intentioned, you run the risk of creating dialogue that is comical or racially insensitive. Simply write what you want the characters to say with all of the words spelled correctly, and let the actors do the rest.

Do not number scenes. Numbers are only used in production drafts and are inserted by the production management team.

CHAPTER 9

Jobs for Television Writers

SPEC SCRIPTS

If you want to work as a writer in television, the first thing you will need to do is pen a few spec scripts—sample teleplays that demonstrate your talent, skills, and ability.

You will need to write at least three specs:

- Two should be for shows currently on the air. Since the majority of TV programming consists of ongoing series, one absolutely vital skill for a television writer is the ability to adapt to the format, style, and voice of existing shows. Writing good sample episodes for currently running series is how you demonstrate this facility. When choosing shows to spec, you need to select programs you really like (so that you will write with enthusiasm and passion) and that the industry considers well-written (writing a successful spec for a high-quality series will demonstrate that you have the potential for true excellence, something writing a spec for lesser program will not show). The series you are penning specs for must be currently airing on television (the industry wants to know you are capable of writing the state of the art). If you write a sample for a series that goes off the air, you can no longer use it.

- Your third spec should be an original piece (ideally, a pilot for a show you would one day like to produce) that demonstrates your ability to create original material and showcases your own unique voice.

- Your specs should all be for the same type of show—all sitcoms, all dramas, all animation, etc. Most writers are eager to demonstrate their versatility—their ability to write every conceivable kind of material. They feel this will make them more marketable ("Look! I can write anything!"), but it actually makes them less so. As is the case with actors and directors and everyone else, the entertainment industry "types" writers: if someone displays the ability to write action well, then he or she is typed as an action writer; those who do good "funny" are typed as comedy writers; and so on. If you demonstrate an ability for writing a certain type of show well, you will have a "brand" that will make it easier for agents to sell you ("You need a sitcom writer? I have the perfect person for you!") and therefore more likely they will want to rep you. It will also make it more likely that producers will hire you, because they don't have to spend precious time and money finding out if you are up to the task ("I need an action writer. You are an action writer. You've got the job!"). So it behooves you to specialize, especially when you are first starting out. You can branch out later, after you are established and successful and a known quantity.

Once your specs are ready, you can begin seeking work.

FREELANCING

Most writers working the in entertainment industry are freelancers. The only exceptions are those writers working on the staffs of ongoing television series.

If your area of specialization is TV movies or miniseries, then you *have to* freelance, because all of these projects are one-offs. These sorts of jobs are obtained the same way feature film writing assignments are obtained: a producer or studio or network executive reads your writing samples (spec screenplays are the best samples for longform jobs) and, if they feel you are right for a project, invite you to come in and pitch your take on the material. If they like your approach, you are given the assignment.

Although most of the writing on television series is staff-generated, freelance opportunities are available. As mentioned in Chapter 4, the Writers Guild of America requires all shows produced by signatories to its Minimum Basic Agreement—which include all the major U.S. studios, networks, and television production companies—to give a certain number of assignments to freelance writers each season. The WGA does this to provide a way in for new writers to break into the industry and to provide access for veteran scribes who do not currently hold a staff position.

The assignments are awarded by a very specific formula: for shows with orders from networks for more than six episodes, the production company must take story pitches from outside writers for all episodes that have not yet been assigned to staff writers at the time the order is placed, although the company is not obligated to buy any of these pitches. For shows with a network order of 13–21 episodes, the company must take pitches for all unassigned episodes, or it can hire a minimum of two freelancers to write two stories—based on ideas pitched by the freelancers or on concepts created by the staff—with options for teleplays. For shows with orders of twenty-two episodes or more, the company must take pitches or hire a minimum of three freelancers to write three stories with options for teleplays, one of which must be exercised.

As with all other writing jobs in the entertainment industry, a freelance series assignment begins with your specs. You submit your samples to a showrunner, either through an agent, through a contact, or directly, if you happen to know the showrunner and he or she invites you to do so. Some series have open submission policies, which means you can send a spec in "over the transom" without knowing someone on the show, but they are rare.

If the showrunner likes your samples, you will be invited to pitch him or her some story ideas. If you are invited to pitch, it is imperative that you prepare for the meeting as thoroughly as you can.

- Begin by knowing the show you are pitching inside and out—the premise, the setting, the characters, the kinds of stories the show tells, the style and structure it uses to tell them, and so on.
- Come up with four or five really good ideas for stories that are suitable for the show and develop them as fully as possible—work out the beginning, the middle, and end, as well as all major plot twists. Create B stories for each concept. Have a clear idea of the themes and points of each story, and know how the events of each involve and affect the show's regular characters. Write your ideas down (in one clear, concise paragraph each) and practice pitching them verbally (so that you don't have to read off the paper as you pitch, which can be awkward).
- Obviously, your ideas should be original—don't propose stories that are similar to ones the show has already done. Production companies are required to provide prospective pitchers with synopses of previous episodes, as well as the series bible (an overall guide to the show—the concept, characters, narratives, etc.). Study these documents well, so that you avoid offering repeats.

If the pitch goes well and the showrunner decides to use you, you will be offered one of several opportunities:

- Story Only: You will be contracted to write a detailed story outline for an episode (based on one of your pitches or a staff-generated idea the showrunner wants to develop).
- Story with an Option for a Teleplay: You will be contracted to write a detailed story outline. The showrunner then has the option to have you develop the story into a teleplay or to give it to a staff writer to develop.
- Story and Teleplay: You will be contracted to write a detailed story outline and then develop it into a teleplay (a first draft and a revision).
- Teleplay Only: You will be given a detailed story outline that has already been developed by the show's writing staff and contracted to transform it into a teleplay.

If things go well, you may be asked to pitch more stories or write more scripts for the show in the future. Or you may be asked to join the staff.

STAFF WRITERS

There are essentially three levels of staffers on a typical television series. The first is actually called:

Staff Writer

This is an entry-level, probationary position—beginning writers are hired on week-to-week contracts, with six-, ten-, twenty-, or forty-week guarantees. During this time, the beginners are given the opportunity to learn the ropes as the showrunners assess their performance and decide whether to hire them on a permanent basis. Staff writers are paid a (relatively) small salary, are not paid any extra fees for the scripts that they write, and do not receive screen credit.

Story Editors, Consultants, and Writing Producers

Permanent members of the writing staff (usually contracted on a season-by-season basis, with screen credit guaranteed) go by many titles, although the job description is essentially the same for all of them: permanent staffers write teleplays (for which they are paid standard industry fees over and above their salaries). They also work with the other members of the staff to devise and develop narrative arcs, story ideas, and detailed story outlines. They read and comment on all the show's scripts and help do rewrites and polishes.

The titles permanent staff members go by are usually determined by the amount of experience they have in the industry, the length of time they have been on a particular show, and their seniority relative to the other members of the staff. Beginners are given the title story editor (or story consultant). they can move up to become an executive story editor (or executive story consultant), and then co-producer, producer, supervising producer, and finally co-executive producer.

Some veteran comedy writers opt not to work full time on a sitcom staff, but will instead come in one or two days a week to help "punch up" a script by adding more jokes and gags. These folks command high fees and are usually given the title script consultant or executive script consultant.

Showrunner

In years past, the showrunner was called the head writer, which is an accurate (if only partial) description of the job, although these days the official title is executive producer.

As previously mentioned, the showrunner is the person responsible for the creative direction of the series. He or she is often (but not always) the creator or the show and determines what sort of stories the series will tell and the style in which those stories will be told. The showrunner assembles and supervises the writing staff and works with the staff to develop the show's ongoing narrative arcs and to devise the stories for each individual episode. He or she meets with freelance writers to hear pitches and decides which, if any, to buy. The showrunner hands out the script assignments, gives notes on every draft, and, as mentioned previously, usually does the final rewrite or polish on every teleplay the show puts into production. He or she approves the casting of all guest actors, supervises the production staff to make sure all the practical and technical elements of the show come together, gives notes to the directors to ensure the script is being properly interpreted, and approves the final edit of each episode. The showrunner is responsible for delivering the show to the network on time and on budget, and deals with the production company, the studio, and the network on all matters ranging from show orders to talent relations to advertising and promotion to censorship issues.

Being a showrunner is an enormously difficult and challenging job, but for television writers, it's a career pinnacle.

CHAPTER 10

Creating a Television Series

It is the dream of just about every aspiring or working television writer to one day create her or his own series.

The opportunity to develop your own show—to dream up your own concept and your own characters and then bring them to life in accordance with your own vision—is a thrilling creative prospect. It can also be a very lucrative one—the creator of a successful television series can earn hundreds of thousands of dollars while the show is in first run on a network, and has the potential to earn millions more once it goes into syndication (when the rights to re-run the series are licensed to hundreds of independent stations across the country and the world) and is released on home video.

In the past, the opportunity to create a series was usually given only to successful, established writers—to scribes who had proven themselves as showrunners or as important contributors to a hit series. In recent years, however, some production companies and networks have been more open to letting less established writers and even people who have no prior experience in television writing try their hands at developing shows.

To create a series, the first thing you need to do is come up with a great idea. In television, a great idea for a series is one that:

- Is clever and entertaining.
- Has characters an audience will like and/or can invest in.
- Is reasonably original. TV is a very conservative business. Although some outlets (primarily some of the premium cable channels) welcome adventurous programming, most networks prefer variations on existing genres and concepts rather than wholly new concepts. Cop shows, medical dramas, legal series, family sitcoms, and workplace comedies are the most common recurring favorites. "The same but different" tends to be the industry's motto.
- Can be produced practically on a reasonable budget. In other words—a show that focuses on character, behavior, and dialogue in a handful of settings and that doesn't depend on numerous locations, a cast of thousands, big action, and a ton of effects.
- Can generate many episodes—anywhere from six to twenty-four a season—over many seasons. The dream of every producer is to get a show that runs for at least one hundred episodes, which is considered the optimal number for profitable syndication.

Once you have dreamed up your idea, you will need to present it to potential buyers.

In the United States, television shows are manufactured by television production companies. Some of these companies are independent, some are divisions of the major film studios, and some are divisions of the television networks. Production companies makes deals with writers (sometimes independently, sometimes through a writer's own production company) to develop ideas for series, which are then presented to the various networks. In industry parlance, a network is any company that transmits television programming. They include traditional networks such as CBS, NBC, ABC, Fox, and the CW (organizations that broadcast over the air through a nationwide affiliation of local TV stations), cable channels such as HBO, Showtime, USA, AMC, and FX (outlets that distribute their shows through a collection of local cable providers), and streaming services such as Netflix (companies that deliver programs directly to their subscribers over the Internet).

If a network likes an idea, it pays the production company (which in turn pays the writer) to develop a pilot script. A pilot is a first episode—a story that establishes the show's premise and introduces its regular characters. If the network likes the teleplay, it will commission the production company to cast and shoot the pilot. If that turns out well, the network will then order a complete series (usually in batches of six, thirteen, or twenty-four episodes) from the production company, with the network paying the production company a license fee for each episode it orders. The production company uses these license fees to cover the cost of making the series. If the cost exceeds the amount collected through the license fees, the company must pay for the overrun out of its own pocket.

In exchange for the license fee, the network gets the exclusive right to air the episode a certain number of times. After that, all rights to the series revert to the production company, which is then free to sell the show into syndication, license it to streaming services, release it on home video, etc. The production company keeps all the money it makes from these ventures, which it shares with any profit participants, including (usually) the writer who created the series.

So, to sell an idea for show, a writer must first pitch it to a production company and then—along with the production company—to a network.

There are many ways to pitch an idea. Writers who have development deals with specific production companies or who have close relationships with production company or network principles may pitch an idea informally. Writers without these deals or contacts may need to make a more formal presentation.

A formal presentation can include a written series format: a document that lays out the premise of the show and identifies what the ongoing central conflict of the series will be—in other words, that explains where the drama is going to come from week after week. The format should describe the regular characters and indicate the roles they will play in the series. The format should also detail how the episodes will be structured—including the number of acts (if any) the show will be presented in and if there will be a teaser or a tag—and describe the style of the show's storytelling: if the narrative is going to be presented in straightforward fashion or if there will be flashbacks, cutaways, narration, and so forth.

A formal presentation should also include either a detailed outline of the show's pilot episode or a complete teleplay, as well as a list of ideas for future episodes to demonstrate the concept's potential as an ongoing series. Finally, a formal presentation should include a crisp verbal pitch for the concept that you can present when meeting with potential buyers.

If the network likes your idea, then you will be paid to write the pilot script (or the pilot script will be bought from you if it already exists). If the network likes the teleplay and orders a pilot, then you will be responsible for doing all necessary rewriting and polishing to get the script in the best shape possible prior to shooting. If the network orders a series and you are an experienced writer/producer, you will become the showrunner charged with generating all of the necessary episodes. If you are not an experienced showrunner, a veteran executive producer may be brought in to help you run the series or to run the show himself or herself, with you in a subordinate position.

If you are running the series in any capacity, once production gets under way, you will be responsible for preparing a "bible"—an expanded version of the format that outlines the show's basic concept, characters, and style—that will be given to all prospective writers to help them get oriented to the program. You will also be responsible for hiring a writing staff and getting a sufficient number of teleplays into work as quickly as possible.

The writer who creates a series and pens the pilot script will receive a "Created By" credit on every episode of the show. If the series is an adaptation (of a book, a movie, an old TV series, etc.), the creator receives a "Developed By" credit (such as Larry Gelbart did on *M*A*S*H*, which he adapted from the novel by Richard Hooker). On occasion, a new writer is brought in to rewrite a pilot script that didn't work in its original form. In this case, the original writer receives a "Created By" credit and the rewriter gets a "Developed By" credit.

CHAPTER 11

Writing Other Forms of Television

Of course, drama is not the only form of television programming, and the others also use writers, if not to the same extent.

News and Commentary

On a television news program, a team of writers—usually including and often headed by the show's anchor—prepares a script for the anchor to read on air that includes any stories the anchor is reporting personally, as well as introductions to the live or prerecorded stories reported by others.

The content of a live or prerecorded news story is usually shaped by the segment's producers, reporter, and editor. Any necessary writing (introductions, interview questions, narration, etc.) is usually done by the producer and/or the reporter, although an outside writer is sometimes used.

On commentary programs, members of the show's writing staff (including the host) pen the text of the commentaries and may prepare questions for the hosts to ask when interviewing guests.

News writers are usually journalists rather than dramatists and so tend to come to television from newspaper or magazine reporting, or from journalism school, rather than from the world of entertainment.

Talk Shows

The writers on a talk show—one of whom is usually the host—write the host's opening monologue, devise comedic bits and sketches, and come up with questions for the host to ask the guests.

Because the primary task of a talk show writer is to create jokes for the host's monologue, many of them come to scriptwriting from stand-up comedy—either as performers or as joke writers for other comics—as well as from dramatic writing.

Game and Competition Shows

On game and competition shows, the writers' primary task is to come up with the questions the contestants must answer and the challenges they must engage in. The writers also craft the host's introductory and interstitial material and provide jokes for him or her to use when interacting with the contestants.

Reality

The conceit of a reality show is that it is a documentary—fly-on-the-wall footage of real people in real situations, presented as it happens with no editorial interference. This is, of course, not the case—the "real-life" drama presented in these series is as carefully shaped and plotted as that in any fictional program.

Some reality shows simply put a group of diverse people (who will hopefully cleave and/or clash) into a very specific situation designed to generate drama (e.g., living together in the same house) and let the cameras roll. Others dream up scenarios for the cast members to enact (one Kardashian sister plays a prank on another; the cast of *Duck Dynasty* attends a high society ball; Ozzy Osbourne tries to make a piece of toast, etc.) that will hopefully produce some entertaining fireworks. Still others write full scripts complete with dialogue for the stars to memorize and perform. These programs are usually filmed the same way that fictional shows are, with scenes being shot over and over again in multiple takes, until everything comes out right.

The ways reality programs are put together also vary, but in general, once the footage for a particular episode has been shot, it—along with transcripts of the talking-head interviews that punctuate the action—is turned over to one of the show's story editors. A story editor (sometimes called a story producer) is a writer/editor whose job is to craft a narrative from the many hours of footage shot for each episode. There are several levels of story editors—assistant story editor, story editor, sometimes a senior story editor—all of whom work under a supervising story editor (a.k.a. head of the story department).

The story editor reviews the transcripts and the footage and highlights the good stuff. He or she then lays out a proposed storyline beat by beat on index cards and pitches it to the supervising story editor for approval. Next, the story editor writes a brief outline, which is given to the supervising story editor and the show's producers for their input. Once the outline is finalized, the story editor writes out a detailed script and puts together a "stringout" (an initial assembly of the footage that will be used in the show, assembled in order according to the script). The script and stringout are reviewed, tweaked, and finally approved by producers, after which they are turned over to the show's editor, who puts the final episode together.

Variety and Award Shows

Variety shows (programs featuring a mix of sketch comedy, song-and-dance numbers, and specialty acts) were once a staple of American television, but are now a rarity. Today, the genre is represented primarily by award shows, which usually contain most of the elements of a traditional variety program along with the trophy giving. The writers on variety shows are responsible for penning the host's opening remarks, the introductions to each act (and, in the case of award shows, each presenter), comedy bits and sketches, and concepts for the song-and-dance numbers. On award shows, the writers are also responsible for devising jokes and banter for the presenters.

As with the writers on talk shows, many of the writers for variety shows come to the genre through stand-up comedy and joke writing.

Documentaries

The content of a television documentary is shaped primarily by the project's producer, director, and editor, although a writer may be brought in to script any required introductory material and narration.

How-to Shows

How-to shows are programs that provide viewers with information they need to accomplish tasks in various areas (cooking, home and auto repair, exercise, etc.). The writer's task on these programs is to take this information, break it down into simple, easy-to-understand pieces, and then work with the experts to formulate visually interesting actions to illustrate it. The writers must also pen explanatory dialogue for the host that sounds natural and is easy for the audience to understand.

Makeover Shows

Whether the focus of the show is on transforming houses, cars, or people, the writers on these programs generate the explanatory material that introduces the subject of each episode, with a strong emphasis on explaining why the subject needs the makeover and how he or she hopes it will change their lives. (In crafting this material, the writers make sure to amp up the drama every step of the way.) They then work with the show's experts to devise makeovers that are highly visual and dramatic and then write a concluding segment that underlines how amazing and life-altering this makeover has been for the subject. The writers also devise the host's introduction and provide quips the host can work into the banter he or she conducts with the show's subjects.

Clip Shows

Clip shows are programs that consist mostly of footage culled from other shows. These shows use writers to pen the material that introduces the clips, as well as any comments or jokes the host or hosts make regarding them.

CHAPTER 12

The Business of Television Writing

THE WGA

The Writers Guild of America, West, and the Writers Guild of America, East, are two separate but affiliated labor unions. The WGAW represents all screenwriters in the United States, as well as television, radio, and new media writers who live west of the Mississippi. The WGAE represents television, radio, and new media writers who live east of the Mississippi.

Together, the two unions jointly negotiate and enforce an employment contract with the majority of motion picture and television producers in the American entertainment business. This contract, called the Minimum Basic Agreement (the MBA), establishes minimum fees and rates of compensation for all big and small screen-related writing jobs and services. (Members are free to negotiate higher rates for their services if they can, but can never receive less than these minimums.) The WGAs also determine the writing credits on all movies and television shows produced by its signatories, collect and distribute residuals, administer a health and a pension plan, negotiate and enforce creative and other rights, and sponsor education, outreach, and advocacy programs.

Each writing assignment with an MBA signatory company earns a writer a certain number of points toward membership. (The number of points varies depending on the assignment: a teleplay for a thirty-minute program is worth six points, the teleplay for a sixty-minute program is worth eight points, and so on.) After accumulating twenty-four points in a three-year period, the writer is eligible to join one of the WGAs.

MBA signatories cannot employ non-WGA members on their projects (unless those writers agree to join the union once they are eligible). Since all the major television production companies and networks are MBA signatories, if you want to work in the mainstream television business, it behooves you to join the guild as soon as you are eligible. Once you become a WGA member, you cannot work for non-signatory companies.

PAYMENT

As previously mentioned, the WGAs' Minimum Basic Agreement establishes minimum fees and rates of compensation for all television-related writing jobs and services. Those minimums vary depending on the type of network a show is being produced for—for example, the fees and rates for shows on commercial networks such as CBS, NBC, and ABC are higher than those for shows on basic cable.

New minimums are established with each new MBA and increase at prenegotiated rates through the life of the current contract. As of this writing, the minimum payment for a thirty-minute story and teleplay on a commercial network show is $24,183; the minimum payment for a sixty-minute story and teleplay on a commercial network show is $35,568; and the minimum for the story and teleplay of a two-hour TV movie is $71,967. For a full schedule of the current minimums for all TV writing jobs, go to the WGA websites: www.wga.org and www.wgaeast.org.

For staff writers, payment comes in the form of a weekly salary. For scriptwriting assignments, payment is usually made in installments—e.g., for a story and teleplay, the first installment of the fee is paid upon completion of the story outline, the second installment upon completion of the first draft, and the last installment upon completion of the final revision.

RESIDUALS

The fee a writer receives for penning a teleplay is for the script itself and for the right to air the episode made from the script a single time. Anytime the show is repeated after that initial airing, all credited writers are entitled to additional payments. These additional payments are called residuals.

The first repeat on the network of origin brings the writer(s) a specific percentage of the original fee. Each re-run after that brings a lesser amount. Reruns in supplemental markets—syndication, home video, streaming, foreign, in-flight, etc.—bring in different amounts. Amounts and percentages are negotiated in the MBA and vary by format and arena. Some markets pay a great deal, some pay very little—the point is that the writer continues to get paid throughout the life of her or his material.

Residuals come through other avenues as well: show creators receive a payment every time a new episode of the series they created is produced, and a writer who creates an original character (a character who is not one of the regulars) in a teleplay for a series episode whom the show's producers opt to bring back in future episodes receives a payment every time that character appears (even if the originating writer does not pen the teleplay for the new appearance).

COPYRIGHT AND REGISTRATION

It is important to protect your work from theft or plagiarism. You can do this by copyrighting your outlines, teleplays, and formats with the United States Copyright Office and registering them with the script registration services of either affiliate of the Writers Guild of America. Doing this will provide you with dated legal evidence of authorship, which will come in handy should there ever be any unauthorized use of your work. (However, do not put the WGA registration number on the covers of your material—the industry considers this an amateurish practice.)

AGENTS AND MANAGERS

To get a job writing in television, you must first get your specs read by people who can hire you—producers, showrunners, network executives, and so on. This is not an easy thing to do. Most production companies and networks will not accept unsolicited material (material submitted cold by writers unknown to them). They abide by this policy primarily to protect themselves from lawsuits, should they happen to produce a show based on an idea similar to one contained in an unsolicited spec. (This is not an uncommon occurrence, as there are usually dozens of scripts floating around the industry at any one time that contain similar concepts—the zeitgeist works in mysterious ways.) They also use it to cut down the deluge of teleplays they might otherwise receive, as well as to screen out substandard material. Instead, production companies will usually only accept scripts submitted by established managers and agents, which means the first thing writers looking to break into the industry must do is secure representation.

This can also be a difficult task. Some agents and managers are willing to accept unsolicited material from unknowns, but most are not. To break through this barrier, aspiring writers must become adept at crafting attention-getting query letters (and emails) that will motivate reps to request their scripts. They must also work hard at developing contacts—cultivating relationships with industry insiders who will be willing to recommend them and their work. (For new writers, the ability to network is just as important as the ability to spell.)

While securing an agent or manager is crucial, you cannot depend on them to get your career started—in fact, most television writers land their first job without the help of a representative. Once again, contacts are crucial—you need to meet showrunners who will be willing to read your material and give you a shot. The best way to do this is to get a job on the inside. Many successful TV writers got their start working as a personal assistant to a writer or writer/producer, or as a writers' assistant or production assistant on an ongoing series.

STAFFING SEASON

If you are interesting in joining the writing staff of a television series, then you must prepare yourself for staffing season.

Networks order most of their shows for the coming season in the mid- to late spring. Once those orders are placed, the showrunners of the picked-up series immediately begin assembling their writing staffs: showrunners of programs that are already on the air and have been renewed for another year need to replace those staff members who have departed for other opportunities, while the showrunners of brand-new series need to put together complete teams from scratch. Since most fall shows begin shooting in early to mid-summer and scripts are needed well in advance, these staffs must be assembled as quickly as possible. And so staffing season begins—from late March until early May, producers go looking for writers, agents try to sell them, and writers make the rounds, going on interviews and doing their best to impress.

It's a hectic period and one you must prepare for well in advance: your spec scripts must be finished and ready to send out; your representation must be in place (agents are too busy during staffing season to consider taking on anyone new at that time); and it's not the time to go out of town on vacation, especially if you are looking for your first job (showrunners may be willing to wait for known quantities, but they'll never wait for a newbie). If opportunity comes knocking, you have to be standing at the door waiting to open it.

DEVELOPMENT DEALS

If a production company or a network is especially impressed with a television writer's work and thinks that writer

has the potential to create successful shows, they will sometimes sign him or her to a development deal. A writer with
a development deal is given a (large) salary, an office, and
an assistant or two, and in exchange spends his or her time
developing ideas, formats, and pilots for television series
that will hopefully make it to the air and become hits.

PRODUCTION COMPANIES

Writer/producers with a strong track record in creating
shows that make it to air will often form their own production companies, usually with the financial backing of a studio
or other large-scale production entity. Having a company
allows the writer/producer to run several series at once (usually by hiring a co-executive producer to be in charge of the
day-to-day operations on each individual program, with
the writer/producer jumping in on the major creative and
practical decisions for all of them), which is obviously a very
lucrative situation.

Acknowledgments

I would like to thank Janet Iacobuzio, Janet Andrews Molicki, and Alison Locke Nelson for their generous input and assistance with this book. I would also like to thank Andrew Morton and Raymond J. Morton for their technical assistance.

Thanks to John Cerullo and Marybeth Keating at Hal Leonard for sparking this project. Thanks also to my agent, June Clark of FinePrint Literary Management, for her continuing support and encouragement.

My deepest love to my family: Raymond J. Morton Sr. and Rita K. Morton; Kathy, Dan, and Caitlin Hoey; Nancy and John Bevacqua; Kate, Maddie, and Carrie Lutian; Rich and Kendra Morton; William Morton; Ken Morton; Claire and Derek Masterbone; Andrew Morton; and Tom, Lindsey, Erin, Jack, and Sean Morton.

Love and appreciation also to my wonderful friends: Maggie Morrisette; M.F. and Linda Harmon; Carmen and Dan Apodaca; Terri Barbagallo; Dharmesh Chauhan; Jim DeFelice, Gina, David, Eva, and Hugo Fénard; Brian Finn,

Faith Ginsberg; Tara, Kurt, Mia, and Mattius Johnson; Richard H. Kline; Michael Larobina, Alison, John, and Bethany Aurora Nelson; Michelle Mahana; Deborah McColl; Roger Nolan; Tim Partridge; Dr. Gary Pearle; Donna and Joe Romeo; David Shaw; and Stephen Tropiano and Steven Ginsberg.

Finally, 我全部的愛安娜·瑪麗亞·阿波達卡.